TOP CARS

MERCEDES

Lee Stacy

W

FRANKLIN WATTS
LONDON•SYDNEY

First published in 2005 by
Franklin Watts
96 Leonard Street
London EC2A 4XD

Franklin Watts Australia
45–51 Huntley Street
Alexandria
NSW 2015

ISBN 0 7496 6008 2

© 2005 The Brown Reference Group plc

A CIP catalogue record for this book is available
from the British Library

Printed in China

For The Brown Reference Group plc
Editor: Bridget Giles
Managing Editor: Tim Cooke
Design Manager: Lynne Ross
Children's Publisher: Anne O'Daly
Production Director: Alastair Gourlay
Editorial Director: Lindsey Lowe

Credits
Pictures: IMP AB
Text: The Brown Reference Group plc/
IMP AB

Note to parents and teachers
Every effort has been made by the Publishers to ensure
that the websites in this book are suitable for children, that
they are of the highest educational value, and that they
contain no inappropriate or offensive material.
However, because of the nature of the
Internet, it is impossible to guarantee
that the contents of these sites will
not be altered. We strongly advise
that Internet access is supervised
by a responsible adult.

Some words are shown in **bold**, like this.

You can find out what they mean by looking

at the bottom right of most right-hand pages.

You can also find most of the words in the

Glossary on page 30.

Contents

Introduction

The German car maker Mercedes-Benz has a proud history. Its parent company is Daimler-Benz, which was formed in 1926 from Daimler and Benz. Those firms were set up by two pioneers of car making: Gottlieb Daimler (1834–1900) and Karl Benz (1844–1929). Mercedes cars started to earn a good reputation in the 1950s. By the 1990s Mercedes-Benz was making some of the world's most stylish cars.

The Mercedes logo is a three-pointed star inside a circle. It was first used by Gottlieb Daimler in the 19th century.

The 1997 A-Class was Mercedes' first fuel-efficient small car. Its size makes it perfect for parking in crowded cities.

It was helped by its merger with the U.S. company, Chrysler. Mercedes cars are highly innovative. They use cutting-edge technology to achieve performance and safety. Some Mercedes models are already thought of as modern classics. Among these are the luxury S600 and E55 AMG saloons, the C43 AMG estate, the CLK coupé, the A-Class town car and the SLK sports car.

The SLK is a modern classic. This convertible sports car is one of the most aerodynamic models Mercedes has ever built for the road.

A top-of-the-range Mercedes S600 is popular in many places as a limousine for transporting passengers in great comfort. The car has a V12 engine and a top speed of 249.4 km/h (155 mph).

Mercedes S600

During most of the 1990s, the S600 was in a class of its own. Large, luxurious and powerful, it was popular in many parts of the world as a limousine. It was Mercedes' largest production car, with a **wheelbase** of 313.9 cm (123.6 inches). It also had the biggest of all Mercedes' engines. Even though overall weight of the car was heavy, the V12 engine could accelerate the S600 from 0 to 97 km/h (60 mph) in fewer than seven seconds.

Vital Statistics for the 1998 S600

Top speed:	*249 km/h (155 mph)*
0–60 mph:	*6.6 seconds*
Engine:	*V12*
Engine size:	*3,987 cc (243.3 ci)*
Power:	*389 bhp at 5,300 rpm*
Weight:	*2,250 kg (4,960 lb)*
Fuel economy:	*17 mpg*

The steering wheel of the S600 is trimmed with zebrawood from central Africa. Zebrawood is often used to decorate luxury cars.

Milestones

1991

Mercedes introduces the S-Class at the Geneva Motor Show. The range includes models of different sizes, but all have a V12 engine.

1992

The top-of-the-range 600 SEL is given a more efficient 2.8-litre engine. The 'SEL' is dropped from the name of the model, which becomes the S600.

1996

Changes to the S600 include slimmer doors and bumpers painted to match the body.

"The huge V12 engine lets the driver know that the S600 is as fast as it is big. Plunge the accelerator and the car steps away, and the five-speed automatic transmission shifts with precision."

The S600 saloon is often used as a limousine because of its luxurious interior. The car's large wheelbase ensures there is lots of leg room for passengers travelling in the back.

Wheelbase   The distance between the front and back axles.

Specifications

Critics have praised the S600 as being the best and most comfortable car in the world. Because of its modified **suspension** system and its **traction**-control system, it gives one of the smoothest and safest rides of any car of the last 15 years.

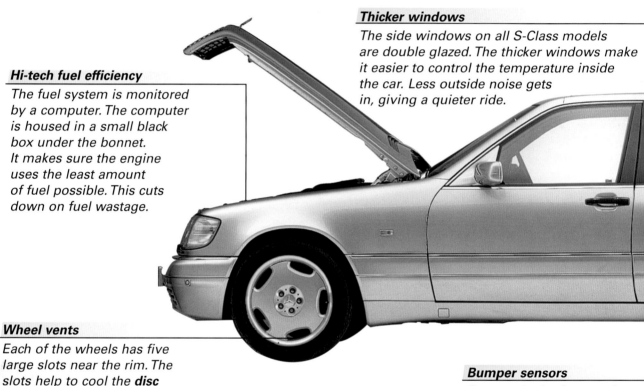

Thicker windows

The side windows on all S-Class models are double glazed. The thicker windows make it easier to control the temperature inside the car. Less outside noise gets in, giving a quieter ride.

Hi-tech fuel efficiency

The fuel system is monitored by a computer. The computer is housed in a small black box under the bonnet. It makes sure the engine uses the least amount of fuel possible. This cuts down on fuel wastage.

Wheel vents

Each of the wheels has five large slots near the rim. The slots help to cool the **disc brakes** inside the wheels.

Bumper sensors

Sensors in the front and rear bumpers detect how far away objects are. They emit sound waves that bounce back off objects. The strength of this echo tells the sensors how far away an object is. The driver can read the distance on a digital display inside the car.

 On most cars, the doors have to be slammed to shut properly. Those on the S600 have electrical motors that automatically close the doors tightly.

The interior of the S600 has many electrically operated gadgets, from a sun roof to rear-view mirrors.

Electronic brake controls

The S600 was the first Mercedes to use an
Electronic Stability Program (ESP). ESP
reduces skidding when the car is turning
a corner or when the road is wet or icy.
ESP controls the balance between the
front and rear brakes and the speed
at which the individual wheels turn.

Disc brakes A brake with a rotating disc
inside the wheel. A clip pinches
the disc to stop the wheel.

Suspension A system of springs that
support a car and make
it travel more smoothly.

Traction The grip between a tyre
and the surface of the road.

Mercedes CLK

In 1998 Mercedes introduced a new **coupé**, the CLK. Designed for sporty drivers, it has some of the best **roadholding** of any Mercedes. It is also very powerful, given that the engine is a fuel-efficient V6. The Mercedes CLK may not be able to reach the top speed of its rivals, the Peugeot 406 Coupé and the Lexus GS 300, but it has better acceleration. It can sprint from 0 to 97 km/h (60 mph) nearly a whole second faster than either.

Milestones

1993

The mid-range C-Class is introduced, with engines of three different sizes: 1.8, 2.2 and 2.8 litres. Only the 2.2 and 2.8 are available in the USA.

1997

The C-Class is expanded to include the C240 and C280. Each has improved engines that are more efficient.

1998

The CLK coupé is launched. It is based on the C-Class and has a V6 engine.

Vital Statistics for the 1998 CLK 320

Top speed:	*240 km/h (149 mph)*
0–60 mph:	*7.2 seconds*
Engine:	*V6*
Engine size:	*3,199 cc (195.2 ci)*
Power:	*215 bhp at 5,700 rpm*
Weight:	*1,475 kg (3,252 lb)*
Fuel economy:	*26 mpg*

Mercedes used ergonomics to design the cockpit and steering wheel. Ergonomics is the science of making things as comfortable and safe to use as possible.

"The CLK is nimble and responsive, with perfectly weighted steering. Ride and handling have been matched to perfection, and the car comes alive with the V6 engine."

One mid-range CLK is the 320 coupé. It has a V6 engine capable of producing 215 bhp. This makes the car perform well at both low and high speeds. Although quite large, the 320 handles like a smaller sports car.

Coupé	A two-door car that usually seats four people.
Roadholding	A car's ability to grip the road without sliding.

Specifications

*The 320 is a mid-range CLK coupé. Although it is only available with a five-speed automatic **transmission**, it rides like a true sports car. The power comes from the V6 engine, which can send the car racing at a top speed of 240 km/h (149 mph).*

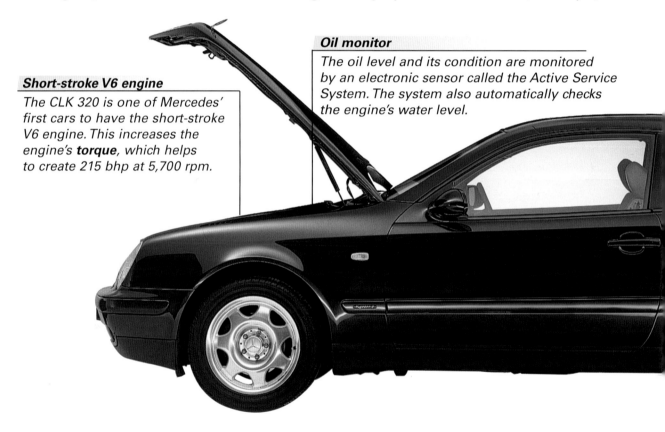

Short-stroke V6 engine

The CLK 320 is one of Mercedes' first cars to have the short-stroke V6 engine. This increases the engine's **torque**, which helps to create 215 bhp at 5,700 rpm.

Oil monitor

The oil level and its condition are monitored by an electronic sensor called the Active Service System. The system also automatically checks the engine's water level.

 The Electronic Stability Programme (ESP) can be added to the CLK. ESP senses when the car is about to lose control. It automatically brakes the wheels and lowers the speed until the car regains control.

 CLK's five-speed automatic transmission detects the road's condition and adjusts gears accordingly.

Controlling wheel spin

The Anti-Skid Control (ASC) on the CLK 320 lowers the engine torque whenever a wheel begins to overspin. This helps the driver to maintain control of the car on wet or icy roads.

Rear headrests

The headrests for the rear passengers are large but adjustable. They are designed for comfort and safety. When adjusted properly, the headrests can reduce the risk of whiplash injury.

Parking mirrors

When parking, the side-view mirrors automatically angle downwards to give the driver better views of the kerb.

Torque The force produced by an engine to rotate the drive shaft of the car.

Transmission The speed-changing gears that transmit power from the engine to the drive shaft.

Mercedes SLK

The SLK is a **convertible** sports car first made in 1996. It was designed to appeal to the upwardly mobile, like its rivals, the BMW Z3 7.9 and the Porsche Boxster. The SLK is one of the most **aerodynamic** road models Mercedes has ever built. To stop the car's body vibrating at high speeds and on rough roads, the SLK is made from a mix of lightweight magnesium and high-strength steel. It also has an excellent suspension system.

Vital Statistics for the 1997 SLK 230

Top speed:	*230 km/h (143 mph)*
0–60 mph:	*7.5 seconds*
Engine:	*In-line four*
Engine size:	*2,295 cc (140 ci)*
Power:	*193 bhp at 5,300 rpm*
Weight:	*1,325 kg (2,922 lb)*
Fuel economy:	*17.3 mpg*

The SLK's cockpit is compact, but still has room for the extra-large steering wheel that is a Mercedes trademark.

Milestones

1954
The first SL sports cars, called the 300SL, are launched.

1994
The prototype for the SLK sports car is shown at the Turin Auto Show. The new model is influenced by the older SL range.

1996
Mercedes begins production of the SLK range. The SLK sports car is an instant success. Demand for the new Mercedes is very high. Critics praise the SLK as a modern classic.

"Drive the SLK as fast as you like on rough roads and it shrugs it off. It doesn't flex and it's not deflected from its path. The SLK is small, yet sporty and fun to drive."

Mercedes made the SLK sleek and aerodynamic. With the top down, the convertible is one of the most impressive-looking sports cars on the open road.

Aerodynamic   Designed to pass smoothly through the air.

Convertible   A type of car that has a top that can be lowered or removed.

Specifications

Mercedes named its sporty convertible SLK after German words. 'S' stands for sportlich *(sporty), 'L' is for* leicht *(lightweight), and 'K' is* kompakt *(compact).* The three words perfectly sum up this modern classic.

Supercharged engine

*The all-**alloy** engine has a displacement of 2.3 litres with four cylinders and 16 valves. The fuel-injection **supercharger** gives the engine high power at all speeds.*

Shatter-proof headlights

The headlights are made out of polycarbonate, an incredibly strong type of plastic that is much harder to shatter than most kinds of glass.

 The SLK was designed so that very little wind affects the driver and passenger when the top is down. There is also a wind deflector behind the headrests.

 A sensor in the passenger seat detects if a child seat is being used. If so, the air bag does not inflate in an accident.

Large wheels

To make the convertible appear more sporty, the wheels are very large. They are 41 cm (16 inches) wide. Fitting over the wheels are even larger tyres.

Choice of transmissions

There is the option of either a five-speed manual or a fully automatic transmission. Most buyers choose the automatic transmission, because it is easier to use but still reacts when the driver is in a sporty mood.

Retractable roof

The hardtop roof on the convertible can be lowered in 25 seconds. Press the button, and hydraulic pumps manoeuvre the metal roof into the boot.

Alloy   A metal that is a mixture of different types of metals.

Supercharger   A device that increases the amount of air in the engine to help it burn fuel efficiently.

17

Mercedes C43 AMG

Mercedes first collaborated with engine designers AMG more than 30 years ago. In 1998 the two firms produced an estate car that was more than a high-class people carrier. The C43 AMG is heavy, weighing 1,564 kg (3,448 lb.), so AMG had to come up with a lot of power. The high-performance V8 engine can send the car racing up to 249 km/h (155 mph). That makes it quicker than **saloons** such as the BMW M3 Evolution and the Cadillac Seville STS.

Vital Statistics for the 1999 C43 AMG

Top speed:	*249 km/h (155 mph)*
0–60 mph:	*5.9 seconds*
Engine:	*V8*
Engine size:	*4,266 cc (260.3 ci)*
Power:	*302 bhp at 5,850 rpm*
Weight:	*1,564 kg (3,448 lb)*
Fuel economy:	*24 mpg*

The interior of the C43 is roomy and comfortable but not very stylish. The cockpit, however, gives the driver total control over the car's awesome power.

Milestones

1967

Hans Werner Aufrecht and Erhard Melcher set up their engine-design company in Grossaspach, Germany. The company's name comes from the initials of the founder's last names, 'A' and 'M', and of the site of the office, 'G'.

1997

After five years of production, the popular C36 AMG comes to an end. AMG and Mercedes had collaborated on the car.

1998

AMG and Mercedes launch the C43 AMG estate car.

"This is no crude V8 conversion; it's perfectly engineered to the very highest standards. The weight balance is improved, and the stiffer, lowered suspension gives incredible handling."

A long wheelbase, a V8 engine and suspension modified from the Mercedes C-Class range make the C43 estate more than just a large people carrier. It is a classic road car.

Saloons   Types of cars with two or four doors and seats for four or more people.

Specifications

For the C43, AMG used the Mercedes C-Class body and **chassis**, but they made major changes to some of the hidden parts of the car. They fine-tuned the suspension, for example, to give a far smoother ride.

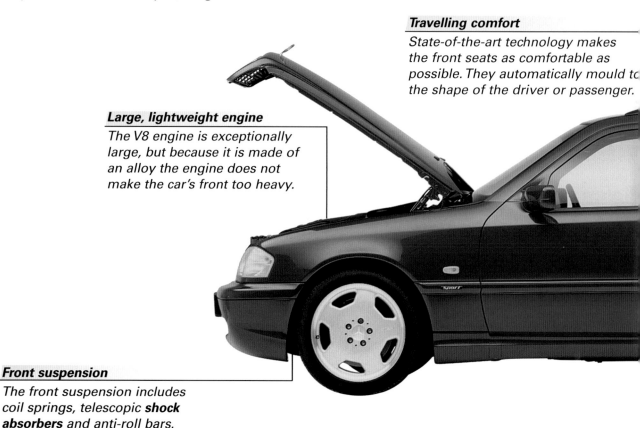

Travelling comfort

State-of-the-art technology makes the front seats as comfortable as possible. They automatically mould to the shape of the driver or passenger.

Large, lightweight engine

The V8 engine is exceptionally large, but because it is made of an alloy the engine does not make the car's front too heavy.

Front suspension

The front suspension includes coil springs, telescopic **shock absorbers** and anti-roll bars.

The AMG V8 engine in the C43 has three valves per cylinder. Two valves take in the fuel, which is combusted by a dual-ignition system. The third valve expels **exhaust gases**.

Mercedes also uses the C43 AMG V8 engine in its off-road, sports-utility vehicle (SUV), the ML430.

Large rear wheels

The rear wheels are 21.6 cm (8.5 inches) wide, while those in the front measure only 19 cm (7.5 inches).

Intense headlights

Xenon headlights are optional on the C43 AMG. They have a gas-charged filament that produces a much stronger beam than ordinary headlights. Mercedes took great care when designing the xenon headlights so that they do not dazzle oncoming drivers.

Chassis	The supporting frame of the car on which the body is fixed.
Exhaust gases	Gases produced by burning fuel in the engine.
Shock absorbers	Springs and other devices that smooth a bumpy ride.

Mercedes E55 AMG

Critics have called the E55 AMG the "fastest and most exclusive sports saloon on the market." Like the C43, the E55 is an engineering and design collaboration between Mercedes and AMG. The car has been around since 1997, and it still has a strong reputation. Fast, high-tech and luxurious, the E55 is an elite car. It has a top speed of 249 km/h (155 mph). Like the Cadillac STS and the Jaguar XJR, the E55 is no ordinary saloon.

Vital Statistics for the 1998 E55 AMG

Top speed:	249 km/h (155 mph)
0–60 mph:	5.4 seconds
Engine:	V8
Engine size:	3,439 cc (209.9 ci)
Power:	354 bhp at 5,500 rpm
Weight:	1,633 kg (3,600 lb)
Fuel economy:	15 mpg

Milestones

1995

Mercedes launches the E-Class as a new range below the S-Class.

1996

In collaboration with AMG, Mercedes introduces the E50, which has a Mercedes body and an AMG engine.

1997

The E55 AMG becomes the latest in Mercedes' E-Class range. It has a powerful 24-valve V8 engine that AMG has designed to be highly fuel efficient and economical.

Mercedes excelled in luxury and gadgetry with the E55. Leather seats and state-of-the-art electronic devices make the inside of the car one of the most stylish ever designed.

"*Well-weighted steering combined with the lowered, stiffened suspension, results in amazingly agile **handling** for such a giant. The massive brakes are among the world's best.*"

The largest model among the E55 range is the estate model. AMG adapted the V8 of the saloon for the estate car so that even though the estate is much heavier than the saloon, it is only 0.2 seconds slower than the saloon when sprinting from 0 to 97 km/h (60 mph).

Handling   The way in which a car responds to the actions of the driver.

Specifications

The electronic gadgetry of the E55 is state of the art. For example, ultrasonic sensors on the front and rear bumpers help to guide the driver while parking. There is also an Electronic Stability Programme (ESP) to keep each wheel from spinning too quickly.

Air bags

For greater passenger safety, the E55 AMG has eight **air bags**. Two of the air bags are located near th front. When inflated they cover th side windows to prevent shattere glass hurting the occupants.

Big, efficient engine

The E55 AMG has the biggest and one of the most efficient V8 engines of any Mercedes. Each cylinder is fitted with two **spark plugs** that fire quickly one after the other. This gives almost continuous combustion.

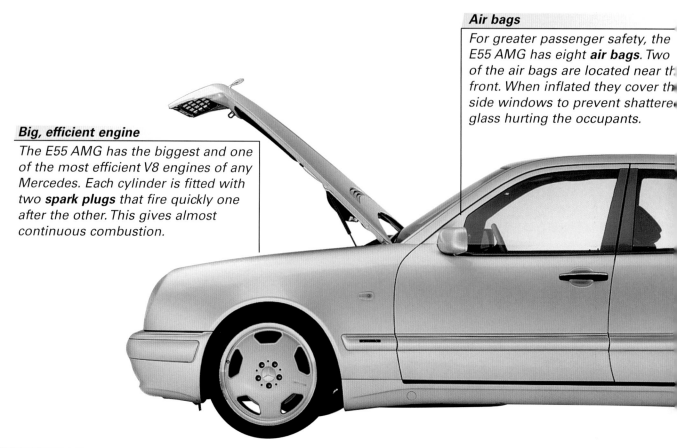

The headlights on the E55 AMG are oval shaped and have polycarbonate (strong, plastic) lenses. There is also a high-pressure washing mechanism that cleans the lenses.

The front and rear wheels are exceptionally large for a saloon. Each wheel is 46 cm (18 inches) in diameter. Inside the wheels are specially fitted vented disc brakes.

Improved suspension

Thicker anti-roll bars and stiffer coil springs and shock absorbers give the E55 AMG the safest suspension system of almost any Mercedes. The changes have not made the car ride any less smoothly.

Hidden front wipers

When not in use, the front windscreen wipers are hidden under the back of the bonnet. The speed of the wipers is adjustable, depending on how heavily it is raining.

Spacious rear seats

The back seats are roomy enough for three passengers to sit comfortably. The headrests also give added protection and comfort.

Air bags   Bags that inflate rapidly in an accident to protect people in the car.

Spark plugs   Devices in the engine that produce an electric charge to ignite fuel.

Mercedes A-Class

At 38 mpg, the A-Class is a Mercedes that takes **fuel economy** seriously. The small and tall A-Class is an unusual shape, but the car's design combines efficient performance with plenty of room for four occupants. Not long after it was introduced, it was discovered that the A-Class could flip over when turning corners at high speed. Mercedes recalled all the models and quickly solved the problem. Today it is one of the world's outstanding small cars.

Vital Statistics for the 1999 A-Class

Top speed:	*180 km/h (112 mph)*
0–60 mph:	*11.1 seconds*
Engine:	*In-line four*
Engine size:	*1,598 cc (97.52 ci)*
Power:	*102 bhp at 5,250 rpm*
Weight:	*1,089 kg (2,401 lb)*
Fuel economy:	*38 mpg*

Milestones

1996

Advertising campaigns begin all over Europe for Mercedes A-Class, even though the car has not yet been built.

1997

The A-Class car is launched, but critics discover that it has major safety flaws. The worst problem is that the car sometimes flips over when making sharp turns. Production ceases and all cars are recalled.

1998

The A-Class is relaunched. All safety issues have been fixed.

Because the engine and transmission are mounted under the car, the A-Class has an unusually large interior for a small car.

"The engines in the A-Class cars are sweet and willing and very economical, thanks to high-top gearing, and the manual gearshift is delightfully short and precise."

Among the most expensive A-Class is the Avantgarde. It gives greater power and sharper handling than other A-Class models. Some critics, however, said it cost too much money for such a small car.

Fuel economy How many miles a car can travel on a gallon of petrol.

Specifications

The A-Class is the perfect city car, able to park in small spaces and easy to drive. It is also a good people carrier, with plenty of leg and headroom. To get such ample space inside the car, the engine and transmission are underneath the floor.

Low-mounted engine
The specially designed engine and transmission are mounted under the floor level of the car to give more room in the tall interior.

Spacious interior
The interior of the A-Class is very roomy for such a small car. Nearly 70 per cent of the car's length is given over to seating and luggage space.

 The front wheels on the A-Class are fitted with very powerful disc brakes. The rear wheels have drum brakes. This is a common combination in many cars.

 The A-Class is not only Mercedes' first small car, it is also the company's first **front-wheel drive** car.

Mercedes appearance
*If you look at the A-Class from the front, with its distinctive **grille**, sloped hood, and three-pointed star badge, it is unmistakably Mercedes-Benz.*

Tall car

For a small car, the A-Class is very tall. It is 158 cm (62 inches) high, and the front seats have 98 cm (38.5 inches) of headroom.

Retractable top

The soft roof can be pulled back to give the occupants an experience similar to riding in a convertible.

Front-wheel drive   A car in which the engine drives the front wheels.

Grille   A grating at the front of a car that lets air in to cool the engine.

29

Glossary

aerodynamic: *Designed to pass smoothly through the air.*

chassis: *The supporting frame of the car on which the body is fixed.*

disc brakes: *A type of brake with a rotating disc inside the wheel mechanism. A clip pinches the disc to stop the wheel turning.*

front-wheel drive: *A car in which the engine powers the front wheels only.*

fuel economy: *How much petrol a car uses over a certain distance, such as miles per gallon.*

roadholding: *A car's ability to grip the road without sliding. Roadholding is especially important at high speeds.*

saloon: *A car with two or four doors and four or more seats.*

spark plug: *Device in an engine's cylinders that produces an electric charge to ignite fuel. The ignited fuel pushes down the piston in the cylinder, rotating the crankshaft.*

supercharger: *A device that increases the air in the engine to help it burn fuel more efficiently.*

suspension: *Spring system that supports a car and makes it travel more smoothly.*

torque: *The force produced by an engine to rotate the drive shaft.*

traction: *The grip between a tyre and the surface of the road.*

transmission: *Speed-changing gears and other parts that transmit power from engine to wheels.*

wheelbase: *The distance between the front and back axles.*

Further Information

websites

www.cyberparent.com/wheels/mercedes.htm
History of Mercedes-Benz

http://auto.howstuffworks.com/engine.htm
How Stuff Works: Car Engines

www.mercedesclub.org.co.uk
Mercedes-Benz Owners Associations

www.mercedes-benz.co.uk
Mercedes-Benz UK

books

● Adler, Dennis. ***Mercedes-Benz: 110 Years of Excellence.*** Motorbooks International, 1995.

● Bacon, Roy. ***Mercedes-Benz in Pictures.*** Motorbooks International, 2001.

● Nitske, W. Robert. ***Mercedes-Benz Production Models 1946–1995.*** Motorbooks International, 1996.

● Sutton, Richard. ***Eyewitness: Car.*** Dorling Kindersley Publishing, 2000.

Index